the 1 thing

What
Everyone Craves—
That Your Church
Can Deliver

by Thom and Joani Schultz

Group
Loveland, Colorado

the 1 thing

Visit our Web sites: **www.grouppublishing.com** and **www.the1thing.com**

CREDITS
Editor: Candace McMahan
Copy Editor: Linda Marcinkowski
Art Director and Book Designer: Jean Bruns
Designers: Randy Kady and Jeff Spencer
Print Production Artists: Lynn Gardner, Stephen Beer, and Tracy K. Hindman
Photographer: Rodney Stewart
Illustrator: Jason Wallengren
Cover Art Director: Jeff A. Storm
Production Manager: Peggy Naylor

Special thanks to Kimberly Butts, Craig DeMartino, Jim and Paula Misloski, Diana Pendley and David Franks of Prestonwood Baptist Church, Steve and Janie Sjogren, and members of Faith Community Church in Longmont, Colorado, for generously assisting with images appearing in *The 1 Thing*.

Unless otherwise noted, Scripture taken from the HOLY BIBLE, NEW INTERNATIONAL VERSION®. Copyright © 1973, 1978, 1984 by International Bible Society. Used by permission of Zondervan Publishing House. All rights reserved.

Library of Congress Cataloging-in-Publication Data

Schultz, Thom.
   The 1 thing : what everyone craves-that your church can deliver / by Thom and Joani Schultz.
      p. cm.
Includes bibliographical references.
   ISBN 0-7644-2728-8 (alk. paper)
   1. Church. 2. Jesus Christ--Person and offices.
I. Title: One thing.
II. Schultz, Joani, 1953- III. Title.
   BV600.3.S36 2004
   253--dc22

2003025029

10 9 8 7 6 5 4 3 2 1   13 12 11 10 09 08 07 06 05 04

Printed in the United States of America.

4

One Hour to Live

Monday, July 22

Today we received the call. It was Betty, our assistant. Her voice trembled.

"Have you heard about Craig?" she asked. Craig DeMartino, our co-worker, friend, and gifted photographer, had been rock climbing yesterday in Rocky Mountain National Park.

So far, this was not unusual. We knew Craig loved to climb. His many years of experience cemented his reputation as a strong, agile, careful, and safety-minded Colorado rock climber. His wife, Cyndy, climbs too. In fact, she's a climbing instructor. Next to spending time with their two small children, there's no place they'd rather be than clinging to the side of a high rock face somewhere.

But something went horribly wrong yesterday afternoon.

Craig and his climbing partner, Steve, decided to scale Sundance Buttress—a vertical granite face in a remote section of the national park. Using all the proper equipment, Craig pulled himself to the top of the climb, while Steve fed him the rope from below.

Steve thought he heard Craig say, "Off belay," giving Steve the OK to let go of the rope. Steve bent over to put on his climbing shoes, in preparation to follow Craig up the cliff.

But there was a miscommunication. For at the same time, Craig yelled, "It's all you," indicating he expected Steve to anchor his rope and ease him down the cliff. In a flash, the coil of Craig's rope near Steve snapped vertical and shot upward.

Steve looked up in time to see Craig falling through the air like a frantic string puppet. With a sickening thud, Craig slammed into the boulder-strewn base of the cliff.

Steve scrambled to Craig's side. The height of the fall raced through Steve's mind. "People die falling that distance," he told himself. That distance was one hundred feet, considered by climbers as the "death zone."

But Craig was still breathing. In fact, he was conscious, but he was critically injured.

Through peculiar circumstances, rescuers quickly reached Craig. But the evacuation from this extremely rugged location chewed up the rest of the afternoon. When the helicopter finally landed at the hospital with Craig aboard, six hours had slipped away since the fall.

Emergency room doctors quickly assessed Craig's injuries. Broken back. Broken neck. Spinal cord 90 percent compromised. Splintered feet and ankles. Internal injuries.

Cyndy rushed to the hospital. The doctor pulled her aside and said that, given all his injuries, Craig may live an hour.

One hour? Come on, God! There lay Cyndy's husband, their two kids' daddy, our friend—unable to move, unable to speak. But still conscious, hearing the doctors' worried words swirling around him.

" ...one hour to live."

What does a person do with an hour to live? What's the most important thing?

Sometimes it takes an extreme, on-the-edge moment like this to startle us into facing what's most crucial in life. Distractions melt away. What once seemed important evaporates.

With one hour to live, what was The 1 Thing Craig needed?

america reeling with shock

farmland in Pennsylvania

'EVIL ACTS OF TERROR'

ACKERS

Millions faced a sobering moment on September 11, 2001. Thousands were killed and injured. Suddenly we felt vulnerable, exposed, fragile, targeted. Mayhem and death seemed excruciatingly close. What would happen next? The agony of uncertainty seemed to suspend the passage of time in an eerie and unfamiliar way.

People began to ask the big questions. What's really important? Beyond the daily grind, the job, the money, the stuff, the prestige--what's *really* important? What's the meaning of life?

The events of September 11 drove millions to plumb the depths of spiritual searching. Churches noted a spike in attendance. Some called it the opportunity of a millennium for churches: to be there, ready, at the very time the masses were desperate for The 1 Thing.

But was the church ready? Church attendance ballooned by 15 percent after the attacks. Then, after a few weeks, attendance receded to normal.[1]

What happened?

We checked with American pollster George Gallup Jr.

96% of Americans polled say they believe in God[2]
41% attend church[3]

Even many of the church-going, however, seem to claim only a thin faith.

Only 13% have a deep and transforming faith[4]

But few are satisfied with a weak faith. The masses crave a deeper faith.

82% desire spiritual growth[5]

So where's the church in all of this?

Two-thirds of Americans polled say most churches are "NOT EFFECTIVE in helping people find meaning in life."[6]

Whoa! Hold on! Most people want to grow in their faith. But most don't feel churches are helping them find real meaning in life.

People are searching. And if the church isn't attracting or satisfying them, they're looking elsewhere. The quest for spiritual moorings is not going away.

This growing hunger for faith and deeper meaning predates September 11, 2001, and other recent scares. A movie in the early '90s probed the populace's search for meaning in life. *City Slickers* told the story of three urban guys looking for something more in life. Mitch, played by Billy Crystal, told his wife, "I just feel lost."

The three guys didn't look for help in the church. They headed out West and joined a wilderness cattle drive-- looking for meaning in life.

Along the trail they became acquainted with Curly, a crude cowboy played by Jack Palance. He'd seen seekers like these before. "None of you get it," he told Mitch. "Do you know what the secret of life is? One thing. Just one thing."

"That's great, but what's the one thing?" Mitch asked.

"That's what you gotta figure out," Curly said.

So, what is it?

What's The 1 Thing?

chapter two

The 1 Thing

So, what is The 1 Thing? (Is it really *just one thing?*)

Is the church delivering The 1 Thing? Why do most people seem to say the church fails to satisfy their deepest longings?

Missing The 1 Thing. How could anyone miss something as big as The 1 Thing? It's not so hard, really. Happens all the time.

In the early twentieth century, the railroads missed their one thing. They passed up the opportunity to join in the development and exploitation of the airplane, which turned out to be far more lucrative than the railroads. Why? They didn't recognize and pursue their one thing. They were too busy running a railroad. But had they realized that their real one thing was *transportation*, perhaps they would have eagerly invested in aviation.

Missing The 1 Thing

As Jesus and his disciples were on their way, he came to a village where a woman named Martha opened her home to him. She had a sister called Mary, who sat at the Lord's feet listening to what he said. But Martha was distracted by all the preparations that had to be made. She came to him and asked, "Lord, don't you care that my sister has left me to do the work by myself? Tell her to help me!"

"Martha, Martha," the Lord answered, "you are worried and upset about many things, but only one thing is needed. Mary has chosen what is better, and it will not be taken away from her."

(Luke 10:38-42)

Luke

So, what's The 1 Thing?

(Check only one.)

❑ Jesus

❑ serving the Lord

❑ proper protocol

❑ justice

❑ a good heart

❑ a growing relationship with Jesus

Jesus? Martha acknowledged and opened her home to Jesus yet was told she didn't get it. Agreeing that Jesus is real is not The 1 Thing.

Serving the Lord? Martha was directly serving Jesus, preparing a meal for him. Yet Jesus told her she didn't get it. Working full speed for Jesus, in ministry for him, is not The 1 Thing.

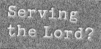

Proper Protocol? Tradition would have required both Martha and Mary to prepare for the guests. But Jesus ruled against the tradition, the ritual, the way things had always been done. That wasn't The 1 Thing.

Justice? Martha argued that she was being unfairly overworked while Mary sat around. Even so, Jesus told her she didn't get it. Equality and fairness are not The 1 Thing.

A Good Heart? Martha had good intentions. Her motives were fine, but she didn't get it. Righteous motives, even in the service of the Lord, are not The 1 Thing.

A Growing Relationship With Jesus? Yes, that's it! That's what Mary chose. She wanted to know and grow closer to Jesus. The Lord was (and still is) looking for friends with whom to develop deep relationships. *That is The 1 Thing.*

The 1 Thing is a heart-to-heart relationship, a close and growing friendship, with God. This is what God craves. This is what we crave. God created every person to yearn for this intimate relationship with him. Nothing else will do.

And without it, nothing else matters. Look at what is perhaps the most quoted Scripture: ➙

> For God so loved the world that he gave his one and only Son, that whoever believes in him shall not perish but have eternal life.
>
> *Jesus*
>
> (John 3:16)

It's strikingly simple. Many have tried to complicate Jesus' message. But his truth remains straightforward. Believe in him and you will have eternal life.

But we must understand *believes in*. This does not mean "knows about." Practically everyone knows about the historical Jesus. Even Jesus' enemies knew *about* him. But they did not *know* him. *Believes in* means to be in relationship with, to trust, to love. Believe, engage in The 1 Thing, and you will have eternal life.

The Scriptures provide many other directions, laws, and teachings. They're all good. But without The 1 Thing, we lose--for eternity.

We heard a pastor say, "I'm not sure it is just one thing." His mental scan of Scripture, his library of theological texts, and his years of seminary training beckoned him to bundle multiple prerequisites. But, like Martha, he may have missed the point of The 1 Thing.

Jesus clarifies for us that our response to his teachings is very important, but nothing is more important than our *relationship* with him. The other factors at work in the Mary and Martha episode-- acknowledging Jesus, serving him, cultivating righteous motives, observing protocol, championing justice--are good endeavors. But the relationship comes first. The other stuff follows and flows out of the relationship.

16

Pilot Training

I'm a pilot. Perhaps the most repeated phrase in pilot training is "Fly the airplane!" Sounds obvious, doesn't it? But flight instructors repeat it again and again for good reason. "Your survival depends on it," they say.

The vast majority of airplane crashes are the result of pilot error. This includes those situations that began with equipment failure or weather problems. Most of the crashes stemming from such scenarios were entirely preventable.

Why then do so many pilots needlessly crash? They get distracted. When problems arise they fixate on the problems, the equipment, the radios, the navigation, the emergency checklists.

And they lose control of the airplane. That's why flight instructors preach, "Fly the airplane!" There's nothing more important than keeping the airplane flying. Without that, nothing else matters.

"Fly the airplane!"

Thom

PHARISEE: "Teacher, which is the greatest commandment in the Law?"

JESUS: "Love the Lord your God with all your heart and with all your soul and with all your mind."

(Matthew 22:36-37)

Like Martha, we can do a good job of performing, but we'll crash without taking care of--first and always foremost--The 1 Thing: a growing relationship with Jesus.

God craves our friendship, our closeness, our intimacy with him. This relationship is the first-and-always-foremost thing he wants.

Ages ago, God had everything. Then he created us people--not because he needed some more creatures. But because he sought companionship. Kin. Friends. Relationship. Love.

God simply craves our love, *more than anything else.*

17

Sunday, August 25

Since the moment we heard the news, we cried to the Lord in prayer for Craig; for his wife, Cyndy; and for their two small children, Mayah and Will.

When we first heard of Craig's condition, we prayed for a miracle of healing. But we also prayed that Craig's relationship with the Lord was good, especially if this was Craig's time to go.

When Craig joined our staff at Group Publishing many years ago, he did not know the Lord. But we watched as God worked through Jesus' friends at Group to bring Craig into relationship with him.

All those friends, upon hearing about Craig's fall, prayed and prayed. We were not ready to say goodbye to our friend and fellow follower of Christ. As it turned out, Craig survived that hour in the hospital. In fact, he made it through the night. And into the next day. Craig's friend and co-worker Bill Fisher managed to get into

Craig's room. "When I walked in, he opened his eyes and saw me," Bill said. "He looked terrible. He had a tube in to help him breathe. He put out his hand, and I grabbed it, and he just looked at me. I told him I loved him."

Later Bill watched as Craig fumbled with a pencil and paper and began scratching a note. Laboriously, he scrawled, "I'm Scared."

"You should be scared," Bill told him. "You're right on the edge of not coming back."

Well, Craig made it through that day. And the next. And the next. Eventually, the feeling began to return to his limbs. He was able to breathe on his own. His internal injuries seemed to just go away. The surgeons bolted his back, neck, ankles, and feet. Given the extent of Craig's injuries and condition upon arrival at the hospital, the doctors cannot explain his amazing progress to this point.

Of course, we know what happened. We are witnessing a miracle. God has chosen to bring his friend Craig through this one.

Today we saw Craig for the first time since the fall.

Before we entered the hospital, we braced ourselves for the worst. We didn't know how Craig would look. But when we entered the room, our friend Craig looked up over his neck brace, grabbed the traction bar above his bed, and flashed his trademark wide smile.

He is so thankful to be alive. We sat and listened to his story, doing our best to hold back the tears.

"A good friend of mine gave me a Max Lucado daily devotion book," he said. "I opened it up to July 21st—the day I fell. The devotion said, 'How far do you want God to go in getting your attention?' [1] To me, the question became 'How far does God have to go to make sure he's number one in my life?' "

He paused, then said, "You know, I would have taken a burning bush or anything. But this is what he obviously felt was necessary to get my attention. Before this happened, I

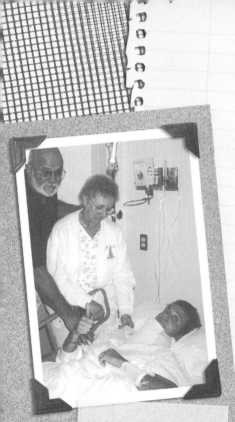

Craig & his parents

was a Christian. I went to church. I did my thing. But I carried baggage. I wasn't putting God first."

Craig gazed out of the window for a moment. "I realize now he cares about your heart."

It's The 1 Thing.

So what does God desire most for his friend Craig? What's God's 1 Thing?

- That Craig enjoys perfect health?

- That Craig works harder for him?

- That Craig masters more biblical facts?

- That Craig knows the historical roots of his denomination?

No, it's a heart thing. More than anything else, God wants a close, loving, trusting relationship with Craig--and with all of us.

A deepened understanding of The 1 Thing now grows within Craig. He's felt how much God craves his love. He's walked with Martha and sat with Mary--next to Jesus.

Luke, through his writing, plops us down in Mary and Martha's house. We get to witness what happens. And we come away with a clear understanding of what's most important to Jesus.

What would happen if we'd plop down in most churches today? What would we perceive? What would seem most important? Would The 1 Thing-- an absolutely unmistakable emphasis on growing relationships with Jesus--shine through immediately? Or would well-meaning but less important stuff distract from The 1 Thing?

What about your church? All week hundreds or thousands of people in your community go about their lives aching for a very special relationship, one that can be satisfied by only 1.

chapter three

"I Have Called You *Friends*"

> crashed 80
> miles southeast of Pittsburgh.
> Passengers aboard the hijacked airplanes began to comprehend the likely termination of their flights. They would not survive. Several reached for their cell phones and quietly dialed their loved ones. If no one answered, they left recorded messages with their final words: "I love you." Interviews with the family, friends and co-workers of passengers

The passengers could have said:
"Be kind to the neighbors."
"Cast my absentee ballot."
"Don't forget the house payment."

But they were focused on their personal relationships. They desperately wanted to say, "I love you."

We'd do the same. When we think of our relationship with our son, Matt, we have many typical parental expectations. But none of those comes close to our deep desire for his love.

Life crises often clarify what's really important. And for parents and children, ultimately

How great is the love the Father has lavished on us, that we should be called children of God! And that is what we are!

John

(1 John 3:1a)

I no longer call you servants, because a servant does not know his master's business. Instead, I have called you friends.

Jesus

(John 15:15a)

As the Father has loved me, so have I loved you. Now remain in my love.

Jesus

(John 15:9)

what's most important is their love relationship.

Our heavenly Father views his children in a similar way. He cherishes the love--the relationship--more than anything else.

Think of it! God invites us to come to him not only as servants and as children, but also as his *friends!*

God the Father sent his Son to live among us, to befriend us, and to show us how to befriend him. We see through his life and ministry a gallery of friendships --all varying in depth and maturity. He built close friendships with Mary and Martha and their brother, Lazarus. When Lazarus got sick, his sisters fully

> My command is this:
> Love each other as I
> have loved you.
>
> *Jesus* (John 15:12)

> If you forgive those who
> sin against you, your
> heavenly Father will
> forgive you. But if you
> refuse to forgive others,
> your Father will not
> forgive your sins.
>
> *Jesus* (Matthew 6:14-15,
> New Living Translation)

expected their friend Jesus to intervene. And Jesus' bond with them showed its depth through his tears and his healing hand.

Jesus developed friendships with his disciples. Some of these friendships were deeper than others. He selected three friends--Peter, James, and John--to accompany him to the Transfiguration and to be with him during his prayer in the Garden of Gethsemane.

And Jesus made the connection between human friendships and our friendship with almighty God.

The formation of healthy human friendships provides clues for our pursuit of The 1 Thing. We make friends with Jesus much as we make friends with other people.

So what's involved in developing a good friendship? We asked our friends and associates to list qualities of and steps toward a great human relationship. Here's what they listed:

- *common interests*
- *shared values*
- *volition—picking your friends*
- *spending time together*
- *talk—give and take*
- *shared experiences*
- *having fun together*
- *eating together*
- *spending time with your friends' friends*
- *sharing emotions*
- *companionship*
- *helping one another*
- *healthy interdependence*
- *love*
- *intimacy*
- *trust*
- *loyalty*
- *willing to sacrifice for one another*
- *forgiveness*
- *commitment*

Take a look at that list, and then consider a growing relationship with God. What can we learn from our human friendships that may contribute to our relationship with Christ? Human friendships can provide an example for a relationship with the Lord.

Notice that some of these qualities fit a parent-child relationship. But some do not. A friend-to-friend relationship ventures into different, often deeper, fathoms of friendship, of fellowship. And that's where God is calling us: into fellowship with him.

We proclaim to you what we have seen and heard, so that you also may have fellowship with us. And our fellowship is with the Father and with his Son, Jesus Christ.

John

(1 John 1:3)

September 14

Today we drove up into the mountains with conflicting feelings. We wanted to hike to the spot where our friend Craig had fallen. We wanted to see for ourselves the setting that changed his life forever.

Craig is still recovering in the rehabilitation center—making progress but experiencing a lot of pain. Though he jokingly offered to lead us to the spot where he fell, we'd have to make this trek without him. The other person who knew exactly where this drama unfolded was Steve, Craig's climbing partner. The one who let go of the rope just before Craig kicked away from the rock wall.

When we asked if he'd take us to the spot, Steve paused, wrestling with powerful emotions of terror, grief, and guilt. He had not returned to the cliff since the accident. This would be a climb like no other. He would be venturing into unmapped personal territory.

He agreed to guide us to the spot.

Steve said very little as we hiked higher and higher toward Sundance Buttress in Rocky Mountain National Park. We wondered what he was thinking as we trudged up the steep approach to the cliff.

Finally we reached the spot. Steve stepped away and seemed to slip into a private, silent conversation with the mountain. He gazed up to the spot—one hundred feet above—where he last saw his friend healthy, intact, vigorous, and strong.

"I've relived this in my mind a hundred times, or thousands, or tens of thousands," he said before his voice cracked. He could no longer hold back the tears.

Steve showed us where he knelt to tie his shoes, thinking Craig would wait for him at the top of the cliff. "He yelled my name," he said. "I turned just in time to see him falling the last fifteen feet to the ground." A tortured look crossed his face. "It was awful."

Last week Craig had warned us that Steve was haunted by guilt. Since the accident he has visited Craig nearly every day. But he can rarely look at Craig without breaking down.

"I told him, 'Steve, this was an accident,' " Craig recalled. " 'You've taken all this guilt on. Let it go, man, because I'm not mad at you. If I go climbing again, I'd go climbing with you the first day, because I'm not mad at you. I think we made a couple of mistakes, small mistakes, that added up to a big one.' "

"If anything, I think he saved my life," Craig told us.

Craig prays for Steve—that Steve can let go of his guilt and can somehow see God's hand in this story. "He's not a believer," Craig told us.

Before we left Sundance Buttress today, Steve recalled all the peculiar "coincidences" that enveloped Craig's fall and rescue.

— Craig hit the ground at an estimated one hundred miles an hour, and survived without brain injury.

— Steve happened to bring his cell phone on that climb ("a freak occurrence in itself," Steve said).

—From that remote spot in the mountains, he got a signal and completed a 911 call.

—Rangers, trained paramedics, who happened to be working in the meadow just below Sundance Buttress, reached the accident scene in thirty-five minutes.

—Two of Colorado's best physicians, a neurosurgeon and an orthopedic surgeon, happened to be on duty to treat Craig on arrival at the hospital.

—Craig's internal injuries, which should have been substantial, just went away.

Steve gazed up at the clouds licking the top of the mountain. "There is some greater power at work here," he said. And with that, we were ready to come down off the mountain.

We see in Craig and Steve the power of friendship, of fellowship, of faith. We see two guys who shared a passion for rock climbing, for calculated risk-taking. A "small mistake" of miscommunication, an imperfection in their interdependence, led to a fall. But grace and forgiveness have prevailed to preserve and even deepen their friendship.

This kind of friendship is vanishing from our busy lifestyles. We find it harder and harder to find, establish, nurture, and rely on real friendships. It's a sign of our times.

We're in a relationship famine. The scarcity of real relationships intensifies our hunger. We crave relationships. We're desperately seeking real friendships. Even as we sit solo at our computers, we graze Web sites that promise to link us with other like-minded people who also seek friends.

> "We're a remote-controlled, security-fenced, internet-commuting, environmentally insulated society. We're increasingly cut off from genuine experiences and expressions of community. We're increasingly removed from real, dynamic relationships. Our high divorce rates, our fractured families, our corporate superstructures and our let's-just-move mindset all evidence our failures at relationships."[1]

Leonard Sweet
PreachingPlus.com

Here lies the real opportunity--and the responsibility--of the church. Jesus calls us to tap into the Mary-like hunger for relationship that calls out all around us.

What if the church prominently fashioned itself around relationship? What if it de-prioritized the distractions of well-intentioned ministries and focused on ending the famine in our culture? What if it elevated human relationship building above the rituals we've come to associate with "church"? What if it utilized what we know about building great human friendships to nurture real friendships with Jesus? What if it made The 1 Thing the top priority?

Most Christians today came to the faith through the relational influence of their friends and families. They met Jesus while pursuing their relationships with other followers. They wanted to belong.

" Four persons in ten say they have been lonely for a long period of time.[2] "

George Gallup Jr.

The world today, as in Jesus' time, hungers for real relationships--with real people and with the real Lord. The world is ready to be invited into a warm, friendly environment where relationships naturally incubate. The spiritually hungry are looking for a *fireside ambience* that lends itself to friend-making.

It's time for a reordering of the church's priorities--on the grand scale of Martha and Mary. It's time to place a Friendship Filter in front of every decision, ministry, program, place, and procedure. It's time to question everything we've been doing for decades.

> Belonging comes before believing.[3]
>
> George Gallup Jr.

Friendship Filter

Question everything. When considering possible options in ministry, ask:

● Which option will best induce and enhance relationships—with others and with Jesus?

● If you were trying to grow a warm, human relationship using one of these options, which one would you choose? (That one is usually the better option for growing closer to Jesus as well.)

● Which option best creates a fireside ambience—a setting that invites relationship building?

● Which option will telegraph to the world that building a close, personal relationship with Jesus Christ is the top priority here?

When applying a Friendship Filter, beware of "yeah, buts." The Martha mentality is epidemic in today's church. Old church dogs resist change. They launch well-rehearsed defense mechanisms and rationalizations. They, like Martha, often operate from a good heart, they cling to proper protocol, and they call on a sense of fairness.

And, like Martha, they're often the busiest servants.

But they're often distracted from The 1 Thing. Distractions have caused the church to evolve into something that looks quite different from the Christian church of Jesus' time.

We humans draw upon what we know. We construct from our own frames of reference. So the church of today bears strange similarities to other institutions we know and have experienced. Rather than emulating Jesus' ministry, which we did not actually see, we've borrowed characteristics that we *have* seen in other familiar settings.

So the church of today often resembles something familiar--such as a police department, a political action committee, a theater, a mortuary, a seminary, or a museum. We'll show you how in the following pages.

It's so easy to lose sight of The 1 Thing.

I loved to sit next to Grandma in church when I was a little girl. She let me look up the hymns in the old hymnal. I loved it when we'd sing Grandma's favorite—number 457—"What a Friend We Have in Jesus."

What a friend we have in Jesus,
All our sins and griefs to bear!
What a privilege to carry
Everything to God in prayer!

Joani

chapter four

Police
Department

The police department enforces the law. It makes sure people follow a long list of do's and don'ts. When lawmakers write new laws, the police officers stand on the front lines to ensure the public's obedience.

We need laws. We need the police. We're thankful for them. Without them chaos would reign.

Some churches seem to really appreciate the police department too. In fact, some have transferred what they know about the police department into their churches. They've made the law and obedience to the law their top priorities, or at least their most visible. They've fashioned their churches after police departments.

When you walk into some church facilities, when you read their bulletins and newsletters, when you observe the obedient majority following the rules, you detect a police department. The do's and don'ts are often the first things you notice. Entire denominations trumpet their rules as their most prominent distinctives. Some even name their church bodies according to their favorite rules.

Favorite Church Rules

- How to baptize
- When to baptize
- Which Bible translation to use
- When to observe the Sabbath
- What to eat and drink
- What to wear
- How to celebrate the Lord's Supper
- Who may partake of the Lord's Supper
- Which musical instruments (if any) are allowed
- What to do with candles, crosses, and flags
- How to address the clergy
- How to dress the clergy
- How women may serve in ministry
- When to stand
- When to kneel
- When to clap
- Who can use the stuff in the kitchen

LINE: DO NOT CROS

Boundaries can be helpful things. But
when the spiritually hungry perceive those
things as the one thing, the church stumbles
over a Martha-like distraction.

My husband, John, and I went through the new-member classes at a church. I was delighted because John was ready to accept Jesus as his personal Savior. But when it came time for a "profession of faith," John didn't use the exact terminology the church members were looking for. Finally, a board member came to us and said the members did not feel comfortable letting us join since John didn't "say the words." It was a humiliating experience, and I had to work with my husband not to allow his heart to be hardened toward God.

Sandy M.

Some rules are good. Some are innocuous.
Others do more harm than good; they're worse
than distractions. They're destructive.

"Walk, Don't Talk"

Today I picked up our two young kids from vacation Bible school at a nearby church. I asked them what they learned. Without hesitation they said, "When you're in a line, walk, don't talk. Look straight ahead and don't play around. When you get inside, sit quietly and don't talk or move." Hoping for something a little deeper, I asked if they learned anything else. "Yes," they said. "If you get up to go to the bathroom, you have to sit in the back and can't get back with your friends."

Tim G.

When rules take precedence over The 1 Thing, people, even small children, see what's really important there. Check out the following signs, actually spotted in churches across the country. What do they telegraph about these churches' priorities? What's their "friendly factor"?

41

Tacked on the walls in every room →

DO NOT TACK OR TAPE ANYTHING TO THE WALLS

**Signed,
The Property Committee**

Fashioning the church after a police department is nothing new. It's been going on for centuries. Check out the religious cops of Jesus' time--and how he responded to them:

NO CHILDREN UNDER 12 ALLOWED IN SANCTUARY.

Age-appropriate classes provided.

Please. . .
NO SOCIAL BEVERAGES IN SANCTUARY

PASTOR PARKING ONLY!

POLIC INE! DO NOT

JC	**Cops**
One Sabbath, the disciples felt a bit hungry, picked a little grain, and ate.	The Pharisees stopped Jesus and cited the law: no grain-picking on the Sabbath.
"The Son of Man is Lord of the Sabbath."	"What about healing? Is it unlawful on the Sabbath?"
He healed a man's shriveled hand.	They plotted how to kill this "law breaker."
(Matthew 12:1-14)	
One Sabbath, Jesus told a disabled man, "Pick up your mat and walk."	"It is the Sabbath. The law forbids you to carry your mat."
(John 5:1-15)	
Jesus and his disciples dined with nonreligious folks at Matthew's place.	"Why does your teacher eat with tax collectors and 'sinners'?"
(Matthew 9:10-11)	

Religious people love rules. Through their actions, some reveal they love rules more than The 1 Thing.

The Lord says: "These people come near to me with their mouth and honor me with their lips, but their hearts are far from me. Their worship of me is made up only of rules taught by men."

Isaiah

(Isaiah 29:13)

Friendship Filter

Remember, developing a relationship with Jesus resembles how we might pursue human relationships. What would happen in human relationships if we used the methods of the police department?

When Joani and I began our relationship, the police department was not the one thing. Now that's not to say we didn't have some rules. And as our relationship moved along, a few more rules began to emerge.

I now know the non-negotiables such as "Always

If a person dropped into your church or into a committee meeting or simply read the signs around your place, what would your rules say about your priorities? What's your one thing--rules or a relationship?

Do your rules enhance or inhibit relationships--with others and with Jesus? Do they create a fireside ambience? Do your rules--or absence thereof--telegraph The 1 Thing, a growing relationship with Jesus Christ?

put the toilet seat down." But I must admit, if Joani had posted little rule signs or enrolled me in a Joani's Rules class, our relationship would have been dead on arrival. I'm afraid I would have viewed her as the Lid Lady who needs to learn how to make her own seat adjustments.

Now I comply without a second thought. Rules have never been our one thing. Love is our relationship's one thing. Love leads us to want to follow the rules, without making the rules the centerpiece.

Thom

> In everything, do to others what you would have them do to you, for this sums up the Law and the Prophets.
>
> *Jesus*
>
> (Matthew 7:12)

DO NOT CROS

chapter five

Political Action
Committee

The competitive world of politics
fascinates some people. Other folks
are simply interested in social
issues. Sometimes they see the
political process as the best
leverage for change. Many of these
people align themselves with

political action committees (PACs)
to influence government and other
institutions.

Some view the church as a log-
ical participant in molding public
policy. In fact, they see political
action as a prime responsibility

of the church. Some of them have been successful in making public issues their church's one thing. Sermons, adult classes, church newsletters, denominational publications, and conferences gravitate toward an agenda of hot topics such as abortion, homelessness, homosexuality, racial injustice, and foreign affairs.

We once belonged to a congregation that had a great affinity for politics. Many of its members were quite experienced in local and state politics and issues. Ed, the associate pastor, devoted countless hours to community action projects.

When the senior pastor retired, the political activists launched a campaign-style blitz to promote Ed to the senior pastor position. His supporters set up petition-signing tables in the church entrance. They peppered the congregation with campaign mailings, complete with catchy slogans. They made campaign buttons and brochures.

Just before the congregational vote on the new senior pastor, the campaign committee promoted "Wear Red for Ed" Sunday. Ed's supporters, and Ed himself, came to church dressed in red—to sway voter opinion toward their "candidate."

He won. We left. They built a congregation in the image of a political action committee.

The world around us can seem riveted on political and social issues. And those issues can often benefit from the influence of Christian folks. But what happens when the church becomes preoccupied with these issues?

We went to one church that always tried to advance one political cause or another. They displayed campaign signs on the church lawn. I remember one sermon in which the pastor talked about the differences between Republicans and Democrats, and how they fit in the grand scheme of good and evil in the world.

Amy S.

When do issues become Martha-like distractions that take away from The 1 Thing?

Congregational and denominational meeting agendas often reveal what's most important for these bodies. If the vast majority of those agenda items seem quite distant from the church's role of growing relationships with Jesus Christ, then it may be time to revisit Mary and Martha.

While reading a church magazine, we noticed an annual summary of one denomination's district assemblies. Here's a list of topics that the church's delegates discussed and voted upon in one round of meetings:

- *A response to racism*
- *Becoming more multicultural*
- *Same-sex unions*
- *Ordination of gays and lesbians*
- *Sexuality studies*
- *Poor and vulnerable populations*
- *Federal child nutrition programs*
- *Needs of elderly people*
- *Churchwide evangelism strategy*
- *Advocacy for people living in poverty*
- *World hunger*
- *Refugee resettlement program*
- *Protecting civil liberties of all people*
- *Israel and Palestine*
- *Advocacy for foreign aid to Colombia*
- *International debt relief*
- *HIV/AIDS*
- *Legalized gambling*
- *Social statement on prisons*
- *War and peace*

Many political and social issues are very important. But what about the masses in our society who desire spiritual growth? What do they most want and need from the church--a conduit that attempts to influence public policy, or the opportunity to personally grow close to the living God?

Any attempt to make political solutions the church's one thing is not new. Some people have always yearned for a political messiah. The elders of ancient Israel came to the prophet Samuel and pleaded, "Appoint a king to lead us, such as all the other nations have"(1 Samuel 8:5).

Many expected Jesus to fill the role of a political messiah who would help them oppose the Roman government.

After the people saw the miraculous sign that Jesus did, they began to say, "Surely this is the Prophet who is to come into the world." Jesus, knowing that they intended to come and make him king by force, withdrew again into the hills by himself.

John

(John 6:14-15)

Jesus didn't come to be a political king. When Pilate asked directly about that, Jesus said, "My kingdom is not of this world"(John 18:36a). Reforming government was not The 1 Thing for Jesus.

Rather than lobby the government, Jesus did spend part of his time personally curing social ills. He healed the sick, caused the blind to see, and fed the hungry. But what was his purpose? His interactions with his friends Mary and Martha provide the clues.

Lazarus, the brother of Mary and Martha, fell ill. "This sickness will not end in death," Jesus said. Why? "It is for God's glory so that God's Son may be glorified through it"(John 11:4). Jesus positioned this coming miracle not so much as a response to a physical problem, but as an opportunity to deepen The 1 Thing.

Before Jesus reached Bethany, the village of Mary and Martha, Lazarus died. Jesus told his disciples, "Lazarus is dead, and for your sake I am glad I was not there, so that you may believe. But let us go to him" (John 11:14b-15). Again, we see Jesus' purpose--that they would believe, that they would deepen their relationships with him.

As Jesus approached Lazarus' tomb, he wept with Mary. That's what friends do.

Just before Lazarus walked out of the tomb, Jesus said, "Father,

I thank you that you have heard me. I knew that you always hear me, but I said this for the benefit of the people standing here, that they may believe that you sent me" (John 11:41b-42). It's always about The 1 Thing--to grow relationships with him.

We see Jesus' priorities again later in Bethany. Mary poured a pint of expensive perfume on Jesus' feet and wiped his feet with her hair.

Judas objected. "Why wasn't this perfume sold and the money given to the poor?" he asked. "Leave her alone," Jesus said. "You will always have the poor among you, but you will not always have me" (from John 12:1-8).

It's all about the relationship--The 1 Thing.

To be clear, Jesus certainly advocated feeding the hungry, clothing the naked, tending the sick, and visiting the imprisoned. He beckons us to love others. In so doing, we show our love for him. Our compassion grows out of our relationship with him.

Service to others is one of the things Jesus' friends do. But service--even directly serving the Lord--is secondary to The 1 Thing, as Martha learned.

Friendship Filter

What happens when the pursuit of social issues takes precedence over developing a relationship with Jesus? What happens when that order of priorities rules human relationships?

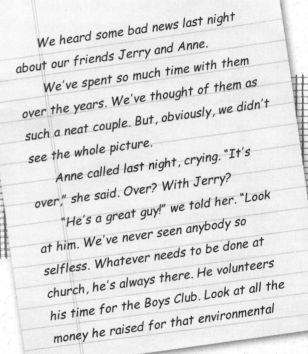

We heard some bad news last night about our friends Jerry and Anne.

We've spent so much time with them over the years. We've thought of them as such a neat couple. But, obviously, we didn't see the whole picture.

Anne called last night, crying. "It's over," she said. Over? With Jerry?

"He's a great guy!" we told her. "Look at him. We've never seen anybody so selfless. Whatever needs to be done at church, he's always there. He volunteers his time for the Boys Club. Look at all the money he raised for that environmental group. He leads the mission trip to Mexico every year. And nobody's written more letters…"

"Yeah, I know, he's a great guy," she interrupted. "But I finally realized that he was so busy doing his things that there was never time for us. I don't know him anymore. And I know he doesn't know me anymore. In the midst of doing all this good stuff, we've just drifted apart."

We cried with her as she told us her plans to leave Jerry. "I need a real relationship," she said.

What are the issues in your congregation or denomination? What weight do they carry? How much attention do they command, versus the time spent, like Mary, at the feet of the Lord?

Of all the needs in this world, what's The 1 Thing the church is best equipped to address?

chapter six

Theater

We like the theater. The stage. The stars. The spectacle. The throngs of theater lovers. A good show provides an absorbing escape from reality, if only for a couple of hours.

For centuries the theater has entertained the crowds. And the basic formula remains unchanged:

- The theater is largely a spectator event.
- The action takes place on the stage.
- Most shows are highly scripted, rehearsed, and predictable.
- Stars provide box office draw.

What's the theater's key objective? To fill seats. Anyone knows a successful theater is one that attracts a big crowd for every performance. The hottest shows fill the big venues. The producers may or may not identify with the essence of the show. But they obsess over "filling the house" with theatergoers. That's the bottom line.

Most people are quite familiar with the theater. And some church folks have transferred their knowledge of the theater to their churches. And their churches are looking more and more like theaters.

In fact, what many would call today's most successful churches actually appear very theater-like. They produce very professional presentations. As on Broadway, audiences passively watch talented speakers and musicians. And "filling the seats" demands constant attention.

When filling seats becomes a Martha-like distraction, The 1 Thing often doesn't make the marquee. The 1 Thing is a relationship. Relationships germinate one on one. They're not crowd focused. Their purpose is not competitive. No good friend says, "I want you as a friend so I can reach my goal of one hundred friends."

"Raising the Temperature"

The leaders at my church decided to do something about our attendance decline. So they devised a new-member campaign and urged all of us to bring a friend to church.

It was all OK until I walked into the sanctuary on Sunday and saw the membership-progress "thermometer"—positioned in front of, and obscuring, the cross.

Jane B.

Theaters emphasize head count. A friendship emphasizes the relationship. Theaters emphasize what happens on stage. A friendship emphasizes what happens offstage, in the heart.

In theater churches the narrow beam of the spotlight focuses on the stage and on the lectern in Bible classes. The star authorities do all the talking. But today's spiritually hungry aren't seeking stage stars. They're craving real relationships.

A national study on adult Christian education asked respondents to score a list of learning methods. Their responses don't really fit the theater. Here's what they said is "extremely important":

Lecture—3%
Group discussion—40%
Building relationships with others in class—44%[2]

When a relationship is The 1 Thing, a church made in the image of a theater doesn't fit. Theaters aren't designed to nurture personal relationships. They're set up to put on a show, fill the seats, and get people in and out.

Jesus didn't pursue a theater approach to ministry. He spent most of his time developing personal relationships with twelve guys. Though large numbers occasionally gathered to experience his teaching, he didn't shape his ministry around filling seats.

Jesus went about building relationships. He demonstrated that this, unlike a theater show, is not a passive endeavor. He involved people in the process. He wasn't merely an eloquent star speaker for adoring audiences.

> For where two or three come together in my name, there am I with them.
>
> *Jesus* (Matthew 18:20)

He used memorable experiences to introduce and enhance The 1 Thing. A few examples:

- Through a frightening storm on the water, Jesus helped his disciples experience true faith in him.
- To make an unforgettable point about self-righteousness and judgmentalism, he challenged those in the temple to cast the first stone at an accused woman.
- He washed his disciples' feet so they would experience, not just hear about, humble servanthood.

These approaches to The 1 Thing really don't fit the theater model. (When was the last time a theater performer removed your shoes and washed your smelly feet?) Jesus often delivered his messages through participatory experiences. He wasn't a show. He was a relationship builder.

In contrast, theater churches of today prefer safe, predictable stage presentations. Communication of the message is a one-way street--from the person in the spotlight. Theaters don't typically engage the audience in experiences or invite the audience to contribute to the conversation. That would be too risky for a theater.

But in the process of developing a relationship, these practices come quite naturally. Friends do stuff together;

they share experiences. Communication is two-way; it's a give-and-take process.

In Chapter 10 we'll share some examples of churches that incorporate participatory experiences and two-way communication in worship settings.

So what's the approach in your church? Does your ministry bear some resemblance to a theater? What's your definition of ministry success? Do your priorities favor filling seats <u>or</u>

Friendship Filter

If our primary goal is to establish growing relationships with Jesus, we need to remember that the process looks a lot like developing human relationships. So how does the theater setting work for growing a friendship?

Thom and I got to know each other and developed our relationship through our work at Group Publishing. We shared a lot of experiences together. And we spent tons of hours just talking, exchanging our stories. We became best friends.

I'm trying to imagine how the theater model would have worked for us. Let's see...

building relationships? Do your attendees primarily just watch, or do they participate and actually experience the message? Are your messages one-way communication, or do they allow for give and take? Are you entirely scripted and predictable, or do you welcome spontaneity?

Theaters serve a valuable role. But the church is not a theater. The church develops relationships, especially The 1 Thing relationship. That's no staged act. It's the real thing.

- Thom would have done all the talking, while I would have been expected to sit quietly and absorb.
- I would have heard Thom's scripted words, but we wouldn't have been allowed to share any experiences together.
- My questions would have been unwelcome.
- Thom's performance would not have allowed me to get to know his friends.

I would have been just one more face in the crowd, keeping my distance from Thom. He would have put on a good show. But I wanted a relationship.

I'm sorry, but I don't think Thom and I would have come together in the theater.

Joani

chapter seven

Mortuary

Ever notice how some places seem to effuse a certain smell? Once you inhale, the odor and the place become inseparable in your mind.

Fresh-baked cookies and Grandma's house. The smell of new clothes and the first day of school. Cheap perfume and Aunt Mildred's car.

Mortuaries have a certain smell. We can't quite identify it. But it's not a happy smell. It's a smell we've come to associate with solemnity. Mortuaries are serious places. Muted colors. Subdued lighting. Quiet, pensive music.

It's weird, but many churches have a certain familiar smell. They smell curiously like a mortuary. The moment you walk in, your olfactory nerves switch you into solemn mode. And usually the church colors, lighting, and music just complete the embalming process.

And that seems to be just fine with many church folks. Without really thinking about it, they create their churches in the image of a mortuary. It's solemn. It's serious. It's not fun.

When my dad died, I appreciated the services of the local mortuary. The funeral director was properly mournful. He knew just how to act around grieving people. Being solemn was his business. Somehow, no matter how he was feeling on the inside, he managed to put on a serious, solemn face—every day.

Thom

A choir member stood up at the beginning of church last Sunday. He announced loudly, "The choir is being a good example of how to behave." He paused, pointed at the congregation, and said, "Hint! It's important to sit and listen to the organ prelude. People shouldn't chitchat while we're getting ready for worship to begin. Thank you."

Some people applauded. If that had been my first Sunday, I wouldn't have returned.

Doc N.

The mortuary mentality creeps into controversies over worship styles. Musical instruments that would seem out of place in a mortuary become taboo in the church. Clapping along with an upbeat song wouldn't seem right at a funeral, so it gets nixed at church, too.

What's the higher goal? To pursue the solemnity of a mortuary or nurture the relationships needed for The 1 Thing?

At Group Publishing we create Sunday school curriculum. And we've always included a dose of fun in our lessons. We believe people learn more when they enjoy the process. And having fun is a natural part of building a relationship, including The 1 Thing relationship. But not everyone agrees with our formula:

Dear Group Publishing:

I'm returning your Hands-On Bible Curriculum. It caused our children to get too wound up before the Bible story. Their laughter disturbed the women's class down the hall. We don't need that. Our children get enough fun and games outside of church. Here they need to learn to sit still, be quiet, and study the Bible.

Myrtle S.

Myrtle is uncomfortable with the concept of fun at church. For her, it just doesn't fit. We wonder how she might have reacted to Jesus' style of ministry.

- Jesus appreciated the built-in tendencies of children. "Unless you change and become like little children, you will never enter the kingdom of heaven" (Matthew 18:3).

- He embraced celebration. His stories of the lost sheep (Luke 15:7), the lost coin (Luke 15:10), and the lost son (Luke 15:32) all concluded with celebration. Fun!

67

- He performed his first miracle at a party--playfully turning water into wine (John 2:1-11).
- He exhibited a penchant for the zany. At tax time he could have been solemn and serious, but he sent Peter to the lake with these offbeat instructions: "Throw out your line. Take the first fish you catch; open its mouth and you will find a four-drachma coin. Take it and give it to them for my tax and yours" (Matthew 17:27). Fun!

Unlike a mortician, Jesus didn't really go for the smell of death. When Martha feared the stinking body of her brother, Jesus brought life and celebration. When a disciple asked for a delay to bury his father, Jesus said, "Follow me, and let the dead bury their own dead" (Matthew 8:22). And when the authorities nailed Jesus to a cross to die, he fooled them all and sprang back to life.

I have come that they may have life, and have it to the full.

Jesus

(John 10:10b)

Friendship Filter

Think of building a human relationship. How does the mortuary motif fit? Would you use the term *solemn* to describe your typical time together with a good friend?

Would you shun fun? If you wanted to make a new friend, would you say, "Want to go out tonight and have some un-fun?"

If you really wanted to get to know someone, would you say, "Sit still, be quiet, and wipe that smile off your face"?

The mortuary model doesn't work well in a friendship. And it's not suited for a church that wishes to pursue The 1 Thing. But don't misunderstand; we're not saying a relationship, the church, or The 1 Thing relationship itself is all fun. Healthy relationships move through all kinds of times—serious *and* fun.

We're simply saying warm relationships do not fixate on cold solemnity.

We appreciate a good mortuary. But the church is not a mortuary.

A few years ago, our church made the national news when the so-called parking-meter granny was arrested in Cincinnati for putting a dime in a stranger's parking meter so he or she wouldn't get a ticket...[We were] completely unaware that it was technically against a city ordinance...

We gained overnight prominence as the church that "illegally feeds parking meters to show God's love in a practical way." The situation was tense...

I decided to turn on the fun and flip the situation completely...I had T-shirts printed with a picture of our granny behind bars...A caption read "guilty of kindness"...The shirts were the talk of the town. In fact, they made their way onto several nationally televised talk shows.[1]

Steve Sjogren
The Perfectly Imperfect Church

chapter eight

Seminary

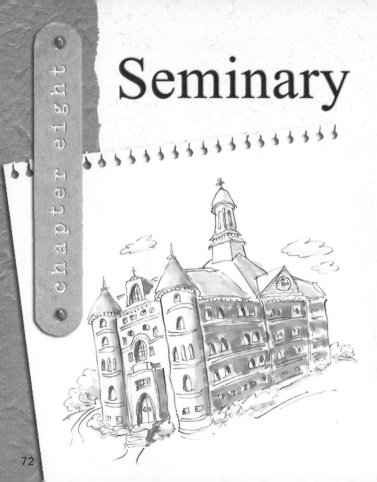

Professors lecture. Students take notes and pore over texts. Facts get memorized. Papers get scored. And placement offices scatter the learned throughout the land.

It's a system that's survived the centuries. It's the seminary.

We need seminaries. They're the keepers of the facts. The good ones do a fine job of transferring information from the haves to the have-nots. They equip the soon-to-be professional ministers with the tools of biblical knowledge, doctrine, and theological reasoning.

Some theological students love the academic rigor. Some do not. But even if they don't relish the learning disciplines, most seem to aspire to the teaching part of the process.

Seminary teaching serves a vital role. Perhaps its importance has caused some churches to seek to emulate the seminary. Their goal becomes akin to the seminary's: to transfer knowledge.

But should that be the church's number one goal? Is that The 1 Thing?

Churches that attempt to be junior seminaries often seem to chase one or more typical Martha-like distractions. We call them "isms":

People who've been through semi-nary, or through a school of any kind, always learn something. Even if they don't learn the curriculum, they learn the hidden curriculum-- the process, the methodology. And they sometimes acquire a certain awe of *information.*

Information becomes something to possess. More is better. Its value becomes self-contained-- knowledge for its own sake. Infor-mation can all too easily become more revered than understanding or application.

Many transfer this ethos to the church. The focus becomes information rather than trans-formation. This system starts early. Take a look at a typical children's Sunday school cur-riculum worksheet:

Word Search

Circle the names of Jesus' ancestors hidden in the puzzle:

H	E	Z	R	O	N	B	O	A	Z
T	R	E	A	B	A	J	E	S	S
U	O	R	M	E	H	B	M	A	R
R	Z	E	F	D	S	A	S	D	A
T	A	P	C	V	H	A	H	O	H
E	S	A	L	M	O	N	I	A	L
A	B	I	U	D	N	A	H	A	Z

Children spend hours toiling over such puzzles in Sunday school. Why? Many Christian educators seem to believe these devices convey Bible information.

But does the investment of time in word scrambles, crossword puzzles, and fill-in-the-blanks draw children into a closer personal relationship with Jesus--The 1 Thing? Would you spend time on similar worksheets if you really wanted to get to know your neighbor across the street?

It's not just children who are subjected to informationism in the church. Many preachers like to hand out sermon worksheets. They look something like this:

"A fool finds _____ in evil _____, but a _____ of _____ delights in _____"

(Proverbs 10:23).

While parishioners are busy taking dictation, the opportunity to bask in the presence of the Lord slips away. Martha would like the busywork of these fill-in-the-blanks. Mary would rather get swept away in the storytelling. She'd rather experience God.

When the focus shifts away from The 1 Thing, information often becomes a panacea, an end unto itself.

The 1 Thing is much more than information about Jesus. It's a relationship with him.

You diligently study the Scriptures because you think that by them you possess eternal life. These are the Scriptures that testify about me, yet you refuse to come to me to have life.

Jesus (John 5:39-40)

Sometimes the consumption of information leads to a hoarding mentality--even arrogance. "I possess more knowledge than you, which makes me superior."

This brand of intellectualism leads some to discount those who may be strong in faith but soft on academic knowledge. Beware of snobbish language such as:

"they check their brains at the door"

"dumbed-down religion"

"anti-intellectual"

"shallow theology"

"they're Bible-light"

These attitudes create the perception that Christian faith is measured by a person's IQ and academic prowess. For some, real religion is reserved for the learned.

Some years ago a fresh, young seminary graduate arrived to pastor a small church in South Dakota. He was determined to share his "superior knowledge" with these "simple folk."

The women of the church invited the pastor to their weekly home Bible study. He agreed--but with one condition: that he alone would share any Bible insights.

So the women sat week after week and quietly listened to the pastor's knowledge. But they soon realized they weren't growing. "We always got so much more out of the Bible studies when we could share our own thoughts," one said.

These plucky women reached their limit when the young pastor proclaimed that Jesus intended the Great Commission for clergy only. He left the congregation shortly thereafter. And the ladies went back to pursuing The 1 Thing.

> For it is written: "I will destroy the wisdom of the wise; the intelligence of the intelligent I will frustrate." Where is the wise man? Where is the scholar? Where is the philosopher of this age? Has not God made foolish the wisdom of the world?
>
> *Paul*
>
> *(1 Corinthians 1:19-20)*

Most seminaries are owned and supported by particular denominations. Or they're aligned with a particular school of theological thought. As a part of their studies, seminarians typically learn the distinctions and advantages of their particular tribe. That's a fitting part of the seminary experience.

But what happens when we emphasize theological brand management in the local church? Take, for example, this sign displayed in front of a church:

WE ARE:
Fundamental
—
Premillennial
—
KJV

What's the goal here? To attract the right people? To discourage the wrong people? (Would most of the community even have a clue about the meaning of these terms?)

Some churches seem more interested in promoting a franchise than in pursuing The 1 Thing. We noticed a letter from a denominational president cautioning his churches to avoid all vacation Bible school programs except the one published by his denominational publishing house. Other programs, regardless of their effectiveness in deepening kids' relationships with Jesus, did not contain enough denominational detail.

Sometimes sectarian parsing takes precedence over The 1 Thing. When we fixate on small differences, we lose focus on the big picture--the relationship. Jesus found this problem repeatedly with the Pharisees and teachers of the Law.

What can we learn from Jesus' approach to ministry? He discounted the Pharisees' prideful knowledge. They pursued what they regarded as theological precision. He viewed it as elitist nitpicking.

> You blind guides! You strain out a gnat but swallow a camel.
>
> *Jesus*
>
> (Matthew 23:24)

Friendship Filter

Becky "loves" Mel Gibson. She's seen all his movies. She devours any magazine that features him. Every night she searches the Internet for new Mel news. She belongs to a Mel Gibson fan club. She knows more information about Mel than just about any other subject.

But does she *know* Mel Gibson? Does she have a real relationship with Mel Gibson?

Becky is a Mel Gibson groupie, a fan, a consumer of Mel Gibson information. Are you a Jesus groupie—or a *friend* of Jesus?

I've known Joani for over twenty years. I love her. And I'm always learning more about her. But it wasn't my mastery of information that brought us together. Our wedding wasn't some kind of final exam. If it had been, I don't think I would have passed.

I might not pass that test even today! There are all sorts of Joani facts I haven't mastered. For example, she has a multitude of relatives. But I can't tell you the names of half of them!

Yes, it's embarrassing sometimes. I'm just thankful she cares more about our relationship than my mental cataloging of her family tree.

Thom

Don't get us wrong. We're certainly not against information. Facts are good. And God, like a good friend, is pleased when we learn about him. Knowledge gathering is a natural and important part of developing and deepening a relationship.

Churches share information about God. That's a good thing. But it's not The 1 Thing.

Love builds up the church. Love--more than perfect knowledge--is the essence of a relationship.

When this love--The 1 Thing--takes first place, a church looks at everything differently. With worship, sermons, curriculum selection, and Bible studies, the emphasis and desired outcome move from information to transformation, from mastery of facts to love of the Master.

> "Americans know all about Jesus but surprisingly few know Him.[2]"
>
> George Barna, researcher

chapter nine

Museum

The small museum in our Colorado hometown is pretty good. You can get acquainted with a lot of dead people. Annie Oakley isn't there, but her gun is. The people who ran the old sugar factory are long dead, but you can see the equipment they used.

Museums remind us of days gone by. They exist to preserve the memories and traditions of the past.

Many churches today have become museums. They exist to preserve the memories and traditions of the past. Some have really excelled at emulating museums. In fact, many old Christian cathedrals are indeed more museums than churches. They attract more who come to soak in the history than those who come to worship.

Tradition can be useful. But when tradition becomes a church's one thing, the church dies. Museum curators in the church cling to all sorts of bygone artifacts--music, worship styles, architecture, furniture, schedules, teaching and preaching styles, the content of membership classes, and on and on. Like relics in a museum display, these things sit unchanged for decades.

Those of us who grew up in the church remember the way things were when we were children. When something new comes along today, we tend to naturally resist it, because it doesn't fit our personal museum mind-set.

No Coffee for You

The worship committee at a church in our hometown discussed how to make the church more inviting, more centered on The 1 Thing. The team noted that people arrived just before worship began and left immediately after the service concluded. Few loitered in the lobby to talk, meet friends, or form relationships.

PROHIBITED

So the committee decided to place a coffeepot in the lobby to encourage people to stick around and enjoy some Christian fellowship. The plan worked. The aroma of fresh coffee lured people to the coffeepot. Once they grasped a cup they tended to hang out, meet people, greet visitors, and talk with friends. The lobby started to become a warm gathering place.

But stop. The church's museum curators became inflamed. Coffee in the entry? This had never been done! This must be wrong. It must be sinful!

The final straw came when a curator spotted someone slip into the sanctuary with a cup of coffee. That was it. The elders called a special, secret meeting at 6 a.m. the next Monday. They voted unanimously to outlaw the coffeepot.

They sent word to the worship committee: "People can drink their coffee in the basement, like they always have—but not in the entrance to the house of the Lord!"

WWED? What Would Elders Do--if they lived in the time of Jesus' ministry? We can just imagine...

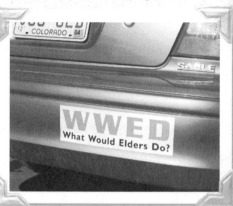

"Hey, you're here to worship God and listen to Jesus preach--not to fill your bellies! You and your five thousand sacrilegious friends, spit out that bread! Hand over that fish! Who gave you that food, anyway? Whoever it was ought to be run out of town."

The church's museum curators have sparked wars in countless congregations. "I hate that new music. What's wrong

Worshipping the Liturgy

Hazel and Harvey recited the same liturgy in the same way for fifty years. It was known as "page 5 in the red hymnal." They knew every word. And they threatened to leave if a pastor even suggested using a newer liturgy.

One Sunday the pastor reprinted the "page 5" liturgy in the bulletin—word for word. Hazel and Harvey refused to participate. That break with tradition—reading the liturgy from the bulletin rather than the red book—was too grievous to be excused. They chose to withhold their worship of God rather than compromise their principles.

with the old hymns?" "The next time they bring those drums in here, I'm leaving." "If the old liturgy was good enough for me in the '40s, it ought to be good enough for you."

For some the church represents the only place where the stress of change need not penetrate. The church becomes a fortress, trying in vain to hold back time itself.

Some church leaders become museums-- personally. They stubbornly hold on to their own old habits and practices, even though their old methods may distract from The 1 Thing.

Ministries dedicated to building relationships with the Lord require many folks to rethink their method- ology. That's too uncomfortable for some. The curator in them won't allow them to move from straight lecture to two-way communication, from "talking on stage" to allowing people to experience a lesson, from being oh-so-somber to being friendly and fun.

The museum mentality is designed to preserve the past, not to grow a friendship with the Lord for today and tomorrow.

Jesus ran into museum curators quite often. The Pharisees loved their old traditions. For example, they held strictly to a tradition of giving their hands a ceremonial washing prior to eating. When they observed Jesus' disciples eating with "unclean" hands, they challenged Jesus.

He said, "You have a fine way of setting aside the commands of God in order to observe your own traditions" (Mark 7:9).

Forget the former things; do not dwell on the past.

God

(Isaiah 43:18)

When the church becomes our shelter from a radically changing world, we fail to turn to God and make him our hiding place and our shelter...When the church becomes a movement and not a monastery, she becomes a place of transformation for the very culture from which we run in fear.[1]

Erwin McManus
An Unstoppable Force

Mrs. Buckingham taught Sunday school for thirty years. Her classrooms always looked the same. Even for first-graders, she lined up the chairs in neat little rows. She stood behind a large podium and recited the Bible stories to the restless children in the same way every week.

One day the Christian education committee members shook her museum. They switched the curriculum to FaithWeaver, a program that uses friendship methods to draw students into relationship with Christ. Mrs. Buckingham saw a lesson that suggested using pillow stuffing and a flashlight to lead the children through a room. The lesson focused on the Exodus 13 story of God leading his people with pillars of cloud and fire. It was an example of experiential Bible learning that children find captivating and memorable.

"I can't do this," Mrs. Buckingham said. "It's just not me. If you're going to use this curriculum, I guess you can't use me."

Keith J.

How does your church appear to the spiritually hungry? They're not looking for a museum. They're craving a relationship. When they first experience your church, what stands out? Do they sense a fireside ambience or a musty museum?

Stephen, a friend from Oklahoma, heard us speak about the power (for better or worse) of a church's culture. We had mentioned that people pick up cultural clues the moment they walk into a church. He had an ah-ha moment. "Oh, no," he said. "We're a museum! The first thing people see when they walk into our church is a wall of pictures—of dead pastors!"

The portraits were someone's idea of a nice tribute to former pastors. But to the spiritually hungry, this church valued its bygone era above the fireside ambience of The 1 Thing.

Are the ministries of your church positioned to protect the past? Or are they thoughtfully arranged to encourage friend-making—with God and with others?

Bubba can't shake the past. He's forty years old and still trying to exist in his high school years.

He still wears his high school football jersey. He still cruises around town in the same old pickup truck he drove in high school.

Everyone avoids Bubba. They're tired of hearing about his old football conquests, his old girlfriends, and his senior drinking parties at the beach.

Bubba has lots of memories, but no friends.

chapter ten

You've walked with us down the street and visited several places that do not develop The 1 Thing. They are Martha-like distractions. The church is not a police department or a political action committee or a theater or a mortuary or a seminary or a museum.

All those places serve important functions and can look good. But we must be careful here, as Jesus was with Martha: "Only one thing is needed." It's a matter of priorities. We may need to say no to some good things in order to say yes to The 1 Thing.

So how do we go about shaping the church around The 1 Thing? Since The 1 Thing is a relationship, let's look at a process of developing a friendship. We can think of four simple parts of that process:

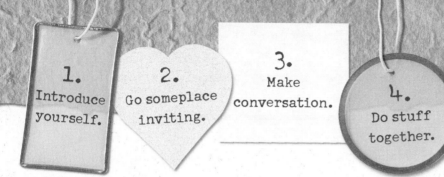

1.
Introduce
yourself.

2.
Go someplace
inviting.

3.
Make
conversation.

4.
Do stuff
together.

These steps toward friendship can lead to lifelong commitment. Wouldn't you naturally do these things if you wanted to make a friend? Let's see how the church can use these four aspects of friend-making to make The 1 Thing first and foremost in everything.

1. Introduce Yourself

Shake your old paradigms of church evangelism. Think like a friend.

If the church is to succeed at The 1 Thing, we need to get better at basic friend-making. That begins with simple introductions.

Jim Misloski ministers at a 1 Thing church in Fort Collins, Colorado. He discovered a natural way to introduce himself and the Lord to his neighbors. Literally, his neighbors.

"I was sitting in my living room one day," Jim said, "and I realized I don't know the people who live right around me. I drive by these people to go to church. I drive past them to go to Mexico to tell people about Jesus!"

What one thing would I encourage all church leaders to do in order to penetrate their communities with the Gospel?

Simple: Each and every church leader needs to build at least one strong, deep, authentic and caring relationship with an unchurched person in his community. Hang out together. Golf together. Go to dinner and movies together. Come out for his son's soccer game; invite him to your daughter's piano recital. Build a vibrant, no-strings-attached friendship. Talk with him about matters of the heart late into the night.

Learn to love this person who's so far from Christ. And when you care about his eternity so much that it's breaking your heart, ask yourself: What can my church do to help me reach this one friend with the Gospel?

Lee Strobel
Outreach magazine

Convicted, Jim drew a map of his neighborhood, filling in the names of any known neighbors, their kids, even their pets. He wasn't able to name many of them. Then an idea hit him. Maybe this map, if completed, would make a welcome gift--and friend builder--in his neighborhood.

So, on Halloween, he and his young children took his blank map and visited all twenty-two homes on his street. He introduced himself and explained he wanted to put together a neighborhood map and directory. If everyone would provide names and phone numbers, he'd give everyone a copy. They all loved the idea and gladly supplied the names of everyone in their households, including their pets.

"We were serving the community with something useful," Jim said. "The level of relationship in the neighborhood really went up."

Later that winter, a major snowstorm buried the area. Jim grabbed his neighborhood directory, called all the neighbors, and invited them to his house for chili and hot chocolate. Fifteen neighbors came to dinner.

Before they ate, Jim announced he organized the impromptu gathering for three reasons. "First, we're snowed in! Then, I wanted to give thanks to God for the moisture. And I wanted to introduce to you our newest neighbors who just moved in--Kate and Jeremy."

Then Jim led the neighbors in prayer. "Nobody batted an eye," he said. They ate, and everyone learned who Jim's greatest Friend is.

Jim was simply being a good neighbor, introducing people. That's how many friendships begin, including a friendship with Jesus.

2. Go Someplace Inviting

We enhance friend-making when we go someplace inviting. We tend to enjoy one another's company more when we're in a pleasant environment.

Yes, it's true that relationships can grow in many settings, even harsh ones. But think about it. Where would you choose to go to get acquainted with someone? We'd choose someplace inviting such as a nice restaurant, a beautiful spot outdoors, a warm living room, or near a crackling fire. We wouldn't pick someplace stark, stiff, ugly, or uncomfortable.

Now think of the church environments you've experienced. What do these settings communicate? Do they invite people to build friendships?

Churches that concentrate on The 1 Thing look carefully at their physical environments. They scrutinize everything: colors, lighting, textures, furniture, seating arrangements, background music, aromas, food, and drinks.

A church near us recently added space to its existing facility. But rather than follow old habits, the leaders planned space in the lobby area for conversation. They invested in comfortable, overstuffed chairs and sofas, arranged in conversational groupings.

Before the expansion, people hustled in and out of worship. Now they linger before and after, sipping gourmet coffee and building friendships.

This is definitely an inviting place!

Many churches have added coffee bars to their entry areas. Some church leaders, however, cringe at the thought of allowing coffee into the sanctuary. That would break an old rule, might endanger the carpet, and just wouldn't seem reverent. But how does that mentality work with 1 Thing relationship building?

Sharing Coffee With Jesus

I know, some of you are gasping for breath right now. "Coffee in the sanctuary! That would never fly at our church." I had that same reaction when this idea first surfaced, but there is nothing more powerful in changing the atmosphere of your church than to allow coffee (with lids!) into your sanctuary. Some would say, "But what about the carpet? We'll soil it." Coffee is a community-building drink. No matter what possible mess is created (we've allowed coffee for years and have had very few accidents), it's well worth the trouble for the atmosphere that is created.[2]

Steve Sjogren
The Perfectly Imperfect Church

1 Thing churches understand the natural bond between food and relationships. They acknowledge that Jesus often delivered his message in an atmosphere of food and drink--on a hillside with five thousand worshippers, in the home of a tax collector, in the Upper Room with his disciples.

Who made the rule that food and drink do not belong in the house of the Lord?

Grace Place, a 1 Thing church in Berthoud, Colorado, puts the hospitality of food and drink right up front--literally. When this church moved its ministry to the main street of this small town, it built a café as the first impression. The Lighthouse Café occupies the prime storefront location.

Patrons walk through the spacious café to get to the worship center and other church space. The restaurant serves sandwiches, soups, salads, lattes, and baked goods Sunday through Friday. It's become a cool place for townspeople to gather. And its fireside ambience attracts not only the physically hungry but also the spiritually hungry. Sunday

Lighthouse Café

worship attendance has tripled since moving to this location with the café.

Creating a fireside ambience may look a little different for various groups within the church. The leaders at Prestonwood Baptist Church in the Dallas, Texas, area built a new children's wing with kids' tastes in mind.

Each week the children go downstairs to the gathering room. But to make the environment kid-friendly and inviting, the children's ministry team installed a large, enclosed, twisting slide that swiftly deposits the kids onto the floor below. They love it!

Before installing the slide, the ministry leaders noticed that many kids arrived late for children's programs. Now they arrive early. They don't want to miss their sliding grand entry. And they bring their friends because church is cool.

3. Make Conversation

Friendships develop when people talk--in an atmosphere of give and take. Nobody grows a real relationship when one person does all the talking.

For many churches, communication of the gospel is a one-way transaction: dispensed from the pulpit to the passive pew-sitters below. But what happens when we employ a friendship filter to the communication part of church ministry? Just as in a good friendship, we have a *conversation*.

1 Thing churches encourage conversation through first-person storytelling, person-to-person talk, and communication with God through lavish prayer time.

FIRST-PERSON STORYTELLING

Most preachers love to preach. Many are pretty good at it. They often tell stories about real people. But what if those real people told their own stories, firsthand?

Lending part of the sermon time to others to tell their faith stories encourages friendships--with God and with other worshippers. Listening to peers tell about their encounters with God carries great power. It's like what happens when friends sit around the fire and relate their stories. They needn't be great orators. They just need to be authentic.

Authenticity builds healthy relationships.

When worshippers hear their peers talk about how God is moving in their lives, the authenticity of their stories makes faith contagious. It's pure word-of-mouth advertising, which anyone will tell you is the most effective.

Many 1 Thing churches bring first-person stories into the worship setting through the use of video clips. They record a person's story, edit it to a pungent two or three minutes, and project it on a screen. Worshippers find these vignettes riveting, they get to know the people on the screen, and they grow more intimate in their relationships with the Lord.

PERSON-TO-PERSON TALK

In 1 Thing churches, the person upfront doesn't hoard the communication of God's love; it's shared. As in a friendship, we learn more and grow in relationship when everyone has a chance to talk.

Who made the rule that sermon times must be monologues?

For years now, our own pastor, Glen Schlecht, has devoted part of his sermon time to person-to-person talk. At certain points in the message, he poses a thought-provoking question, asking listeners of all ages to talk it over with the folks next to them. He might ask a question such as "When is it hardest for people to forgive one another?" He then asks volunteers to share something from their conversations. He takes what he hears and weaves it into the rest of his message.

Such sharing accomplishes several things. It involves everyone. Nobody dozes when conversing with a partner. Everyone has to think. Everyone has to personalize the message.

Sharing thoughts with a partner not only enhances learning and understanding, it nurtures the relationship with the partner. That's good if the partner is a family member; it provides a time to talk about faith issues. If the partner is a stranger, that's good too. It provides a time to start a relationship with a new friend.

This person-to-person talk may need to be introduced carefully to a congregation. From time to time, Glen says something such as "In order for you to get the most out of this

After trying interactive sermons when I got the congregation involved—through pair-shares or active exercises—a couple came into my office to register their concern. These types of messages made them uncomfortable. They preferred for me to just speak and them to just listen.

I asked for examples of which sermons they didn't like, and they told me in great detail what it was I had preached about on the days I used interactive sermons. They couldn't remember what I had preached about in sermons when I simply preached, but they sure liked those better.

Doc N.

Scripture, I'm going to give you a chance to talk about it."

Growing a relationship isn't always comfortable. Comfort is not the goal. Growth is the goal. And often a relationship requires some challenges in order to grow.

Person-to-person talk causes 1 Thing growth throughout a church's ministry, especially in Christian education settings. When people are allowed to contribute to the conversation, they learn more, remember it longer, apply more of it to their lives, and build more relationships.

Learner-to-learner faith talk is a 1 Thing distinctive we've embedded in all the curriculum and Bible studies from Group Publishing. It works with all ages and results in deeper relationships with Jesus and with others.

Conversation is also the active ingredient in small-group ministries. Small groups provide natural settings for 1 Thing relationships to grow. Person-to-person talk brings people closer to one another and to Christ.

> It is in small groups that people can get close enough to know each other, to care and share, to challenge and support, to confide and confess, to forgive and be forgiven, to laugh and weep together, to watch over each other, and to grow together. Personal growth does not happen in isolation.[3]
>
> Gilbert Bilezikian
> Community 101

LAVISH PRAYER TIME

Good relationships require plenty of talk time. It's no different when developing a relationship with God. 1 Thing churches set aside significant chunks of time for believers to talk with God.

Many churches rush through prayer time, especially any time designated for God to speak. That quiet time often gets pinched to just a few seconds. Why is that? Perhaps it's the leaders' haste to get to the "good stuff"--the sermon and the music. But today's spiritually hungry long for quiet time. In their hectic schedules, they find precious little time to simply sit and listen for God's gentle voice. Isn't it appropriate for a worship service to provide ample time for a conversation with the Lord?

Prioritizing The 1 Thing also means engaging congregation members in lavish prayer outside of regular worship services. At Jim Misloski's church, mentioned earlier, members gather every Wednesday night for fifty minutes of concentrated prayer. Members share their concerns, joys, and dreams.

"Our prayer time is fresh, desperate, and persistent," Jim said. "It's like a conversation with God. It's like sharing our needs and joys with the president--but it's better; it's with God!"

A church in California takes its prayer emphasis into the community. Its members are trained to pray before meals in restaurants. But they add a powerful 1 Thing twist: They tell the server, "We're about to pray. Is there anything we can pray about for you?" Waiters and waitresses often break down and cry when invited into a conversation with the Almighty.

Friends grow closer through shared experiences. The same is true in building a relationship with God. In fact, God's been using experiences to bond with his people since the beginning. From the Garden of Eden to the burning bush to the Red Sea to a wedding in Cana to the present day, God has demonstrated that he wants his people to <u>experience</u> him, not simply to know about him.

The church has embraced some God experiences, at least to the extent of engaging in such things as baptism and the Lord's Supper. But what does it look like when a church truly understands the 1 Thing potential of "doing stuff together"?

Westwinds Community Church in Jackson, Michigan, regularly uses experiences in worship. In his book *Morph!*, Westwinds pastor Ron Martoia describes how his team used desert references from the Gospel of Mark, such as John the Baptist's work in the desert and Jesus' temptation in the desert. The team wanted the congregation to experience the desert--in worship.

Our worship team creates "hands-on" experiences. Last Sunday we talked about walls that separate us from other people. The design team constructed a wall of cinder blocks down the center aisle.

After the sermon we were given time to pray about any walls we needed to ask God to break down for us. We could write a prayer on a piece of paper, tear it up, and place it in an offering bowl at the cross. Or we could actually remove a block from the wall and place it at the cross.

I knew this experience helped people build relationships with Jesus when I spoke with the mom of six-year-old Zachary. He wrote on the paper the name of another boy with whom he'd been fighting. He took it to the cross, placed it in the bowl, and then asked for help to carry a block to the cross.

After church Zach told his mom that he knew Jesus wanted him to forgive his friend and to treat him better.

Margaret M.

With loads of sand and cactus plants (borrowed from a florist), they converted their worship space into a desert. Worshippers were invited to remove their shoes and take a smooth stone as they ventured onto the sand.

"I was able to biblically paint the picture of how rugged deserts feel in our lives but how important they can be to our formation," Ron writes. "The stones represented their lives and the solitary aloneness we often feel in life."

Worshippers were invited to toss their stones in the middle of the desert. "Placing your rock in the

We ventured into the old London church on a chilly Sunday night. In the glow of a red light, we stepped over what appeared to be an empty frame for concrete. We later learned the theme of the worship was "Christ in the City," hence the concrete motif.

Worshippers knelt on a gigantic map of London and marked with a yellow marker where they'd been during the past week. After discussions in small groups, a black light illuminated the yellow-marked trails on the map, showing everywhere Christ had been represented during the week. It was stunning!

The worship leader then poured wet cement into the form we saw at the entrance. He told the congregation that the new slab, when dry, would form part of a new altar, reminding everyone of the church's mission and witness in the city.

Joani

And I, the Son
of Man, feast
and drink, and
you say, "He's
a glutton and a
drunkard, and
a friend of the
worst sort of
sinners!" But
wisdom is
shown to be
right by what
results from it.

Jesus

(Matthew 11:19, NLT)

middle of the desert and watching the accumulation of hundreds of other rocks during Communion was a reminder that not only did Jesus have an angel minister to him in the desert, but we also have a community we can 'do life with' when things are going tough," Ron writes.[4]

That's a picture of building 1 Thing relationships--with God and with fellow believers--through a shared experience.

So where do we look to design a church focused on The 1 Thing? We look to the process of friend-making that we already know. We introduce ourselves. We go someplace inviting. We make conversation. And we experience things together.

It's really Jesus-style ministry. He modeled these things. In fact, he built quite a reputation for being a friend, even in the face of criticism.

The Son of Man calls us to be his friends and to build friendships with those around us and to invite them into relationship with him as well. That's The 1 Thing.

And you know what? We don't have to know it all. "Wisdom is shown to be right by what results from it." Jesus is interested in results. He wants a close relationship with us. And he wants more friends.

We don't need to be experts. Look who Jesus recruited to carry out his ministry. These weren't scholars or theologians or noted orators. They were regular guys, regular guys who had the ability to make friends. With them Jesus built his church.

It's funny. The "star" ministry leaders today are sometimes called "great communicators." That may be true. But is oratory really the key ability to spreading The 1 Thing? Maybe the key ability is more like match-making. Who Jesus really needs are friends who know how to build a friendship--the most important friendship in the world.

April 30

Craig's fall from the cliff wasn't the end of his story. In many ways it was just the beginning.

He's home, playing with his kids, and back at work—once again creating awesome photographs.

During his ordeal, a film crew documented his story. Today we decided to give a copy of the video or DVD—free—to any church that would use it to grow relationships with Jesus.

We named it After the Fall, a double meaning that ties in with original sin, sometimes called the Fall.

Craig fell through the air like a rag doll. He hit the ground at one hundred miles per hour. He landed upright, on his feet, which was likely the only possible survivable position. Had he crashed on his side, his head, or any other position, he almost certainly would have died instantly.

Park rangers told us that just before Craig hit the ground, the branch of an old pine tree brushed his tumbling body and tilted him in an upright position.

Seeing that pine tree, we remembered that some people refer to the cross as "the Tree."

After the Fall, what saved Craig?

The Tree.

> Greater love has no one than this,
> that he lay down his life for his friends.
>
> *Jesus*
>
> (John 15:13)

CHAPTER 1

1. George Gallup Jr. and D. Michael Lindsay, "Understanding the Times and Knowing What to Do: A Gallup Briefing on Faith in America," a presentation made to Group Publishing, October 30, 2002.
2. George Gallup Jr. and D. Michael Lindsay, *Surveying the Religious Landscape* (Harrisburg, PA: Morehouse Publishing, 1999), 2.
3. Gallup and Lindsay, "Understanding the Times and Knowing What to Do: A Gallup Briefing on Faith in America."
4. George Gallup Jr. and D. Michael Lindsay, *The Gallup Guide: Reality Check for 21st Century Churches* (Loveland, CO: Group Publishing, Inc., 2002), 9.
5. Gallup and Lindsay, *Surveying the Religious Landscape*, 78.
6. Gallup and Lindsay, *The Gallup Guide: Reality Check for 21st Century Churches*, 13.

CHAPTER 2

1. Max Lucado, *Grace for the Moment* (Nashville, TN: J. Countryman, a division of Thomas Nelson, Inc., 2000), 226.

2. Barna Research Online, Goals and Priorities, www.barna.org/cgi-bin/PageCategory.asp?CategoryID=23, June 24, 2003.
3. Barna Research Online, Worship, www.barna.org/cgi-bin/PageCategory.asp?CategoryID=40, June 24, 2003.

CHAPTER 3

1. Leonard Sweet, PreachingPlus.Com, "A Sign or a Son?" August 3, 2003.
2. George Gallup Jr. and D. Michael Lindsay, "Understanding the Times and Knowing What to Do: A Gallup Briefing on Faith in America," a presentation made to Group Publishing, November 11, 2003.
3. Ibid.

CHAPTER 6

1. Steve Sjogren, *The Perfectly Imperfect Church: Redefining the "Ideal" Church* (Loveland, CO: Group Publishing, Inc., 2002), 21-22.
2. Adult Sunday school survey conducted by Group Publishing, Inc., February 2003.

CHAPTER 7

1. Steve Sjogren, *The Perfectly Imperfect Church: Redefining the "Ideal" Church*, 80.

CHAPTER 8

1. George Barna, *State of the Church: 2002* (Ventura, CA: Issachar Resources, a division of the Barna Research Group, 2002), 117.
2. Ibid., 126.

CHAPTER 9

1. Erwin Raphael McManus, *An Unstoppable Force: Daring to Become the Church God Had in Mind* (Loveland, CO: Group Publishing, Inc., 2001), 65.

CHAPTER 10

1. Excerpted from "Community Impact: One Friend at a Time" by Lee Strobel, which originally appeared in the March/April 2003 issue of Outreach magazine. Copyright © 2003 Outreach, Inc. and Lee Strobel. Reprinted by permission. All rights reserved.
2. Steve Sjogren, *The Perfectly Imperfect Church: Redefining the "Ideal" Church*, 125.
3. Gilbert Bilezikian, *Community 101* (Grand Rapids, MI: Zondervan, 1997), 54.
4. Ron Martoia, *Morph! The Texture of Leadership for Tomorrow's Church* (Loveland, CO: Group Publishing, Inc., 2003), 140.

endnotes

Exploring

the

1

thing

at Your Church

"Only one thing is needed."

Jesus

You've read this book. Now you're ready for action: How can your church become intentionally focused on The 1 Thing?

Start by identifying a team: a group of thoughtful leaders and friends from your church. Get a copy of this book for each person on your team. Commit a time or series of meetings to discuss this book and how it applies to your church. Plan for team members to mark up their own books, add to them, and make them their own.

The following pages provide a road map for discussion and discovery. Use them to fuel plans for change in your church's unique situation. Be creative. To allow flexibility, choose options and pacing that suit your team. You may want to plot six consecutive weeks for study, a daylong event, or a weekend retreat. The point? Get people together to grapple with making your church undeniably focused on The 1 Thing.

To enhance your time together (and make it fun for the team),

● *choose a setting that communicates warmth, friendship, and hospitality.* That will subtly help "teach" the Friendship Filters.

● *provide food and beverages.* This is one more way to communicate relationship building, Jesus-style. Choose one person to be the snack bringer, or share "chef" duties with the group. Depending on your time frame, goodies can be low-key, or your meeting times could revolve around a meal. Meet in a restaurant or in homes. Allow time for fellowship. That's part of the process too.

● *begin and close each session with prayer.* No matter how you plan the discussion sessions, seek the Lord's guidance and wisdom. God loves being with his friends! Prayer includes God in your conversations.

■ **FRIENDLY INTRODUCTIONS—**
Begin your team time with introductions and an explanation of why each person is on the team--key leader position in the church, new member, worship leader, for example.

Have people partner up. Explain that we all share one thing in common: birthdays. Allow thirty seconds each for partners to tell about the childhood birthday they remember best. Then have everyone find a new partner and tell about a teen birthday. Switch partners again, and have them tell about a memorable adult birthday.

Tip
Keep this activity moving quickly. (It isn't easy—people love talking about themselves!) This allows everyone to quickly learn more about three others in the group. Often this sparks conversation starters for later friendship-building discussion.

Watch Craig DeMartino's Story on Video or DVD

We've shared our friend Craig's story of tragedy and triumph with you in this book. But we know there's even more power in meeting Craig on video or DVD. We've chronicled Craig's ordeal in a project we call *After the Fall*. We believe God can use Craig's compelling story to influence your church in powerful ways. Visit www.the1thing.com for details.

You'll see references to *After the Fall* throughout this discussion guide. To locate the scenes referred to here, set the counter on your VCR or DVD player to 00:00:00 when the Group logo appears.

■ **ONE HOUR TO LIVE**— Have the group members close their eyes while one person reads the journal entry from Monday, July 22, starting on page 5.

Alternatively, if you have the *After the Fall* video or DVD, watch it from the beginning to 8:02.

Invite people to imagine they have just one hour to live. What would they do? What would they hope for? Have people share this in pairs if your group is larger than six.

Tip

For optimum sharing, always form smaller groups with time built in for report-backs. We suggest if your group is larger than six, always form groups of two, three, or four. That guarantees full participation from everyone. Plus, it models friendship building!

■ **STATISTICS SAY**—Turn to pages 9 and 10 to review the statistics. What surprises you? Focus on the box that says, "Two-thirds of Americans polled say most churches are not effective in helping people find meaning in life." Talk about your church. Talk about the tough stuff. Would people say your church consistently helps them find meaning? Why or why not? What would longtime church members say? visitors? children? teenagers? singles? other population segments?

Friend-Making Idea

Find a time to watch the movie *City Slickers* as a group. Mine it for spiritual insights. Oh! And enjoy munching on some tasty popcorn too! (For extra discussion ideas, consider subscribing to www.ministryandmedia.com.)

■ **VISIT MARY AND MARTHA'S—**
Read Luke 10:38-42 in the box on page 13. Check the boxes you are most inclined to choose. Why is each of the first five answers so typical? Which answer does your church most commonly reflect? Why?

Have each team member individually read the explanations following each possible answer. Encourage each person to circle, underline, star, or jot exclamation points near the words that most resonate with your church concerning a growing relationship with Jesus. Have people show their pages to a partner and tell why they marked what they did then report back to the whole group. Write and draw insights on a poster to hang up as a reminder during future discussions.

■ **WHO ARE WE: MARY OR MARTHA?—**
Draw an imaginary line across the front of the room. Designate one end "Mary" and the other end "Martha." Have people stand along the continuum at the points they think best describe your church. Right now, is it more like Mary or more like Martha? Discuss your discoveries. Does your entire team agree? Why or why not? How will that alignment affect the church's future direction?

■ **DISTRACTIONS, DISTRACTIONS**—No church is immune to distractions. We're still on earth, not in heaven! Form teams, and ask them to list the distractions your church is dealing with right now. After sufficient time, solicit one distraction at a time from each team's list. Draw or write the responses on a "Distractions" poster.

To demonstrate how distractions hinder a church, have one person continually read John 3:16, again and again. One by one, have each person stand and begin shouting words from the "Distractions" poster. All the while, have the reader keep reading. Then one by one, have each person stop shouting.

Talk about what just happened. How did people feel during that experience? How is that like what actually happens in our churches? How do churches obscure the gospel by activities and distractions?

Revisit the research quote at the end of the chapter: "Nearly two-thirds of regular church attenders say they have never experienced God's presence at a service." Ask for reactions to this statistic. What would be the response at your church? What might be required to help people experience God at your church?

Pray for clear vision and purpose for your church.

■ FRIENDSHIP SCRIPTURES—

Review all the Scripture passages in the boxes on pages 25 and 26. Ask participants each to choose the passage that speaks loudest to them about our relationship with God and to explain why. Encourage doodles and drawings that enhance the Scripture.

Search the Bible for words God uses to describe our relationship with him. Form groups and make "relationship" connections. How does the Bible paint a picture of our connection to God? How does a friendship play into each of these? Assign the following Scripture passages to different groups:

Bride, bridegroom (Matthew 9:15; 25:1-13; John 3:27-29; Revelation 21:2).

Brothers (Romans 8:29-30; 12:10; Hebrews 2:11; 1 Peter 2:17). Children (John 1:12; Romans 8:14, 17; Galatians 4:7; 1 Peter 1:14; 1 John 3:1-10). Family (Galatians 6:10; Ephesians 5:21-6:4; Hebrews 2:11).

Father (Matthew 6:9; 2 Corinthians 6:18; Galatians 4:6; Hebrews 12:4-11).

Friend (John 15:13-15). Shepherd (John 10:1-18; 1 Peter 2:25). Vine (John 15:1-9).

Have groups report their discoveries. If you have the *After the Fall* video or DVD, watch from 8:02 to 15:00.

Friend-Making Idea

Swap "best friend" stories. Spend time storytelling. Have the team tell about favorite times with best friends. For fun, institute a storytelling contest with crazy categories such as funniest friend, most reliable friend, I-can't-believe-he's-still-my-friend, and still-friends-after-all-these-years friend. For extra smiles, invent a category for every person's friend! Talk about how Jesus is a person's best friend.

■ **BUILDING A FRIENDSHIP**—Talk about the list on page 27. Add to it. Then review the list, and have people circle the words that best describe how your church operates in the "friend-making" category.

Together choose the three words your church needs to work on most. Underline them. Make another poster containing the three words you all agreed on.

Friend-Making Idea

Worship together. As you focus on your growing relationship with Jesus, spend time in prayer and worship. A great resource for focusing on The 1 Thing is Matt Redman's CD, *The Heart of Worship.* Just having it play as people arrive for your meeting adds a special 1 Thing focus. If possible, sing favorite worship songs as a group.

If you have *After the Fall,* watch from 15:01 to 19:20. Compare Craig's friendship with Steve to our friendship with Jesus. Talk about Craig's realization of The 1 Thing.

■ **FRIENDSHIP FILTER**—Dig into the box on page 35. Have each person jot down an area of ministry in the church he or she is presently involved in. Suggest that each use the questions in the box to scrutinize that ministry in light of the Friendship Filter. Ask everyone to report discoveries to the group.

Conclude this section with a time of confessional prayer. Realize it's so easy to lose sight of The 1 Thing. We get defensive, rationalize, and use lots of "yeah, buts." Ask for God's forgiveness for making other things the one thing. Refer to Exodus 20:3 or Mark 12:29-30.

■ **FAVORITE RULES**—Together review the list of "Favorite Church Rules" in the box on page 39. Reach agreement on which you can cross off because they don't apply to your church. Then add a few of your own rules--written or unwritten.

For fun, go on a walking tour of your church. Pretend you're on "Official Rule Patrol." Make notes of any rules--written or implied--you find. Return to your meeting place, and talk about your discoveries.

■ **JC AND THE COPS**—Form two groups. Have one group read the statements in the "JC" column in the box on page 43 and the other respond with the adjacent statements in the "Cops" column. Have a good laugh, then talk about how those words apply to your church today.

■ **REVIEW WHAT WE DO**—Bring copies of the latest bulletins, brochures, pamphlets, or other materials that represent your church to others. (You'll use these for the rest of the sessions, so keep them handy.)

Use this material to remind your group of everything your church offers. Have team members review all of these ministry areas, programs, places, and procedures.

Then have partners analyze one specific area of ministry to determine whether it has "police department" qualities. Talk about what you discovered. Any surprises?

■ **POLITICALLY SPEAKING**—Place a check mark beside each topic in the box on page 50 that distracts your church. Any to add?

Discuss what you uncovered.

Now have small teams identify the issues that command your church's attention. Assign a different issue to small groups or trios. Have each come up with a "political speech" to convince

Jesus that this issue is more important than a growing relationship with him. Have fun with it. Talk about what you discovered through this process.

■ **"WHATEVER YOU DO..."**—Take an in-depth look at Matthew 25:31-46, especially verses 37-40. When does a church cross the line and become more like a political action committee? Has your church ever done so? If so, when and why?

Friend-Making Idea

Just for fun, build a "campfire" with candles or a string of twinkly Christmas lights. Gather around and use it to set the stage for your small-group sharing. Observe how the "fireside" atmosphere affects the level of conversation.

Surprise everyone by serving S'Mores!

■ **FILLING THE SEATS**—Ask members of your group to sit in a line of chairs, side by side. Facing forward, have participants each tell the person next to them about their day--without ever turning and looking at them. Do this for a minute or so, then stop. Ask them to share what they felt during that experience. How is that experience like or unlike what happens in your church?

Discuss how your church is like a theater. Do people *experience* the message and *experience* Jesus' love when they come to your church? How scripted or spontaneous is your worship service? How have you fallen into the trap of "filling seats"? Next, examine your education ministries. Are they passive or active? Are they communicating The 1 Thing? Why or why not?

■ **HONEY, IF YOU LOVE ME...**—Ever play this old game? The object is to remain stone-faced and *unsmiling* while one person tries to make someone in the group smile. One person goes to another and says, "Honey, if you love me, won't you please, please smile?" The "victim" must remain stoic while saying, "I love you, honey, but I just can't smile." If the victim doesn't crack, the smile-elicitor must go to someone else and try again. Do this for a few rounds. Be ready for some laughs--even though they're not allowed!

Talk about the silly game and how that is like or unlike your church. Is your church like a mortuary? Why or why not? Does your church accept fun and spontaneity, or is it more like a "dead zone"? What prevents your church from having fun?

Friend-Making Idea
Do something absolutely spontaneous together!

Ideas for
CHAPTER EIGHT
Seminary

■ **ISMS**—Form three groups. Assign each group an "ism," then ask each group to read the pertinent section, reflect on the Scripture, and discuss how that particular "ism" affects a friendship with Jesus:

Informationism--John 5:39-40 (pages 74-75);
Intellectualism--1 Corinthians 1:19-20 (pages 76-77); and
Elitism--1 Corinthians 8:1-3 (pages 78-79).

What does your church need to do to combat its "isms"? Use the questions throughout the chapter to spark deeper discussion.

If your church belongs to a denomination, when has your church emphasized denominational distinctives over The 1 Thing?

Conclude this section by "praying" 1 Corinthians 13. Ask God to make your church a haven for people who want to love Jesus and grow in their relationship with him.

Ideas for
CHAPTER NINE
Museum

■ **TRADITION!**—For spice, play *Fiddler on the Roof's* classic song "Tradition." Then ask each person to think of one of your church's traditions. For fun, play Charades, having each person act out the tradition he or she thought of, while the others guess. What surprised you about doing this?

Now discuss ways your church clings to the past. (Remember, your church doesn't have to be very old to have begun collecting items for its museum!) List your church's "sacred cows." How might they hinder friendship? What would help people grow in their relationships with Jesus? What museum item is the most difficult for your church to give up?

■ **SELF-EVALUATION—** Invite each person to circle a point on each line below to create a visual "continuum" that describes your church.

■ **WHERE WE CAN GROW**—It's time to select one or more areas your church can improve to help focus on The 1 Thing. Review and compare the continuums your team just completed. (Refer to the posters you created earlier.) Use your discoveries to

This describes our church:	NOT AT ALL!							COMPLETELY!
Police Department	├──┼──┼──┼──┼──┼──┼──┤							
Political Action Committee	├──┼──┼──┼──┼──┼──┼──┤							
Theater	├──┼──┼──┼──┼──┼──┼──┤							
Mortuary	├──┼──┼──┼──┼──┼──┼──┤							
Seminary	├──┼──┼──┼──┼──┼──┼──┤							
Museum	├──┼──┼──┼──┼──┼──┼──┤							

help choose which areas in your church need the most attention.

Your team can help choose the priority or priorities. By now, you've probably uncovered a hot topic or two. Select one for the following activity:

Have someone role-play a person's first impressions when encountering the aspect of ministry you've identified. Discuss what you uncover. Refer to the four friendship steps on page 91 to evaluate the ministry's present setting and activities.

Spy Cam

If you're game, ask someone to use a hidden video camera to show your team what it's like to visit your church for worship or other activities.

As a team, take a look! For added intrigue, turn off the sound and just watch. What do the visuals tell you about your church's Friendship Filter? Or just listen to the sounds without the picture. What do you hear? What do the sounds tell you about your church?

Use this candid approach as a discussion starter to explore your church with fresh eyes and ears.

Brainstorm specific action to change what you're currently doing. To assure success, make your steps Specific, Measurable, Achievable, Realistic, and Timely--SMART.

You may want to repeat this process for other ministry areas.

■ COMMUNICATE, EVALUATE, CELEBRATE—As you make plans to focus on The 1 Thing, communicate your intentions with others in your church. Don't sabotage your hard work by forgetting to share your insights. Good friends can't wait to tell their friends what they've been doing.

Plan a reunion with your team to assess your church's progress. Schedule a time now to lock it on people's calendars.

Conclude by reading 1 John 4:7-12. Add favorite worship songs, pray for one another, and pray that a growing friendship with Jesus is reflected in all you do.

If you have the *After the Fall* video or DVD, watch the rest of the story, beginning at 23:37, for your send-off.

Once your leadership team is on board, you'll want to get your entire congregation tuned in to The 1 Thing. Everyone needs to know what's most important at your church. And once your members embrace and practice the principles of Jesus-centered friendship, expect your church to grow.

You may wish to plan a sermon series based on Mary and Martha and 1 Thing thinking. We've provided a model sermon series for you on our Web site:

www.the1thing.com

You can have some fun and guide your congregation down the street—discovering the distractions of the police department, the seminary, the museum, and all the rest.

And you may wish to include segments from the After the Fall video in your messages. You'll find the compelling story of this rock climber's accident a riveting tool to help your people focus on The 1 Thing. See www.the1thing.com for information on obtaining your copy of this video or DVD.

One of our Friendship Filters is staying in relationship with you, the reader. We'd love to hear your stories, struggles, and successes. Tell us how your church is living out the Friendship Filter. You may contact us at

Thom and Joani Schultz
1515 Cascade Avenue
Loveland, CO 80538
tschultz@grouppublishing.com
jschultz@grouppublishing.com

May God bless you as you deepen your friendship with him and bring others into an abiding 1 Thing relationship.

Thom Schultz

Joani Schultz